TESTING THE WATERS
Basic Tenets of Faith

ISBN 978-1-949628-19-7
Printed in the United States of America.
10 9 8 7 6 5 4 3 2 1   22 21 20 19

Published by The Pastoral Center, http://pastoral.center.

Developed in partnership with MennoMedia and Brethren Press. Series editors: Fumiaki Tosu, Ann Naffziger, and Paul Canavese. *Testing the Waters*: Writers, Jeff Wright and Lani Wright. Project editor, Lani Wright. Staff editors, Susan E. Janzen, Julie Garber, and James Deaton. Updated design, Paul Stocksdale.

All rights reserved. Purchase of this book includes a license to reproduce this resource for use in a single parish, school, or other similar organization. You are allowed to share and make unlimited copies only for use within the organization that licensed it. If you serve more than one organization, each should purchase its own license. You may not post this document to any web site without explicit permission to do so. Outside of these conditions, no part of this book may be reproduced in any form or by any means, electronic or mechanical, including photocopying, recording, taping, or via any retrieval system, without the written permission of The Pastoral Center, 1212 Versailles Ave., Alameda, CA 94501. Thank you for cooperating with our honor system regarding our licenses.

For questions or to order additional copies or licenses, please call 1-844-727-8672 or visit http://pastoral.center.

Portions of this work © 2019 by The Pastoral Center / PastoralCenter.com. Adapted and published with permission from Generation Why Bible Studies. © 1997, 2015 Brethren Press, Elgin, IL 60120 and MennoMedia, Harrisonburg, VA 22803, U.S.A. All rights reserved.

Unless otherwise noted, the Scripture passages contained herein are from the *New Revised Standard Version of the Bible*, copyright © 1989 by the National Council of the Churches of Christ in the United States of America. Used by permission. All rights reserved.

>> OVERVIEW

When conversing online, the acronym IRL stands for "in real life." The virtual world of social media, text chats, blogs, and more have the power to remove us from the real world. What we experience online can skew our perspective on what it means to be human. It can numb us, incite us, distract us, depress us, confuse us, and make us rude or impatient. Strangely, this supposedly "social" and "connected" technology can profoundly disconnect us from others.

Religious faith can also place us in a bubble, especially when it distances us from others. When we keep the prophetic message at a safe distance, obscured in theological language and abstractions, we are missing the whole point. And when we see our parish as an insider club that serves itself, we can forget the radically inclusive message entrusted to us: God's love is for *everyone*, and God expects us to transform the *whole world* through that love.

Through the incarnation, God showed up in the real world to show us that our faith is not just about talking the talk, but also walking the walk. It can be risky. It can be confusing. It can hurt. But living out our faith can also bring us great purpose, peace, and joy.

This series connects the Bible with the tough questions that youth (and adults) encounter in their neighborhood, in school, among friends, and even online. This process will help you as a leader break open these issues in a fun and meaningful way, sparking conversation and the kind of life change Jesus invites us to embrace.

THE ROLE OF PARENTS

As children enter middle school and high school, they become more independent, self-reliant, and, well, self-centered. This can bring parents to make assumptions that this is the time to step back, giving their child more space to form their identity. While there is truth to that at some level (adolescents definitely shouldn't be smothered), this is a stage of life when parents should in fact *lean in*. The apparent confidence and bluster youth show on the outside can mask the insecurity and confusion on the inside. Youth need their parents to be involved more than ever.

WHOLE FAMILY FORMATION

Parents are the primary teachers of their own children, and parishes are waking up to the fact that faith formation programs need to bring parents into the process if they hope to see faith passed on to the next generation. Recent studies give us more and more evidence that the role of parents is the most important factor in determining whether a child will embrace faith as they move toward adulthood. Research from the Center for the Applied Research on the Apostolate shows that parents who talk about their faith and show through their actions that their faith is important to them are more likely to have children who remain Catholic.

More about Whole Family Formation

To learn more about how your parish can take a comprehensive whole family approach to faith formation, visit **GrowingUpCatholic.com**.

While whole family events with elementary-aged children are on the rise, the role of parents can be an afterthought in youth ministry. We have designed the sessions in this series to work with or without parents present, and we encourage you to offer them as parent-child events.

If you choose to involve parents, it is important to consider before each session how to best do so. Many of the activities in this series are high-energy, creative, or silly. Some parents may need some encouragement to get out of their heads and have fun with the group. A few activities involving physical contact would be inappropriate for parents and youth to participate together, and we have noted them as such.

There are a number of ways to approach discussions with parent participation. Unless you have a small group, you will likely want to break into smaller groups for conversation. Some youth may be self-conscious and unable to be completely honest and open in a group situation with a parent present. For this reason, you may choose in some cases to assign parents to different groups from their own children, or to have separate parent and child groups altogether. Be sure to cover expectations around confidentiality. It is inappropriate for a parent (or youth) to share with another parent what their child said in a small group.

Note that even if parents and their children do not share all conversations together in the session, they will still have a valuable shared experience and can have extended conversations about it later.

THANK YOU

The role you play in gathering, animating, praying with, and forming youth is a valuable one. Thank you for all you do to serve the church and its families!

Bible-based Explorations of Issues Facing Youth

TESTING THE WATERS
Basic Tenets of Faith

>> INTRODUCTION

Navy blue skirt or pants, white shirt, dark shoes, pair of jeans, a tan or khaki jacket. Every wardrobe needs some basics, a foundation for the rest of the closet. Just so with faith; you need the basic outline, tenets of belief.

These concepts—liberation, covenant, salvation, baptism, discipleship, and community—are central to Christianity. They are the navy blue and tan basics of Christian faith. Though we tend to think of them in terms of the church, their roots are in the experience of the Israelites as recorded in the Hebrew Scriptures. Therefore this unit looks first at the basics of God's action to liberate the Israelites from slavery and to make them a community bound in covenant with their liberating God in Exodus.

Then, in the fullness of time, God sent the Son, Jesus Christ, whose faithfulness, even when it meant his death, saved us from ourselves so that we might be a people for others. Once we make a deliberate choice to turn away from whatever separates us from God, and turn toward a life of discipleship, we make a public statement in the form of baptism. Or, in the case of those baptized as infants, our parents make that commitment on our behalf. Baptism marks our embarking on a life of following Jesus in the company of the faith community.

This unit will ferry participants through these six basic tenets of the Christian faith in a roughly chronological look at salvation history and how believers respond to it. This short course on the basics is a way to test the waters (baptismal) of Christianity before diving in. For those who've "passed through the waters," it will be a chance to review basics. As a primer on Christianity, this unit could also be nicely paired with another In Real Life unit called *Mantras, Menorahs, and Minarets*, which looks at basics in other major faiths.

EXTENDER SESSION

Extender sessions suggest special activities related to the issue of the unit. They help accommodate the diversity of parish schedules. Since each unit is undated, participants may study units in their entirety and still participate in special events of the parish that get scheduled simultaneously with Bible study time. Extender sessions can be used anytime, but the one for this unit best follows **Session 1 or 2 (Option A), or after Session 5 or 6 (Option B)**. Calculate now whether or not you will be using the extender session.

THE TEACHING PLAN: The parts of the session guide

- **Faith story.** The session is rooted in this Bible passage.
- **Faith focus.** This is the story of the passage in a nutshell.
- **Session goal.** The entire session is built around this goal. What changes—in knowledge, attitude, and/or action—do you desire in your group?
- **Materials needed and advance preparation.** This is what you will need if the session is to go smoothly. You'll feel more at ease if you've taken care of these details before you meet your group.

FROM LIFE TO BIBLE TO LIFE

The teaching plan we use is called *life-centered*. However, when we write each session, we always begin with Scripture. We ask, what does this particular passage say, especially to youth? Each session moves from life to Bible to life. So the Bible is really at the center of this way of teaching.

In every session we try to hit upon a tough question that participants might ask. Find out what questions on this issue are important for your group. Feel free to bring your own input and invite your group members to add their own experiences.

TEACHING THE SESSION

The five step-by-step movements will carry you from *life to the Bible and back to life*. Each session takes about 45 to 50 minutes. If there is a handout sheet for the session, take note of any complementary activities and stories.

1. **Focus.** This activity is intended to create a friendly climate within the group and to draw attention to the issue.
2. **Connect.** Talking, drawing, role playing, and other activities invite participants to express their own life experience about the issue.
Also use memory, reason, or imagination to get the group thinking about *why* they view the issue the way they do.
3. **Explore the Bible.** With a minimum of lecturing, dig into the faith story and search for answers to questions raised in the first activities. The Insights from Scripture section will help clarify the faith story. Help participants discover how the faith community understands the Bible passage.
4. **Apply** the faith story. This is the "aha!" moment when participants realize the faith story has wisdom for their lives.
5. **Respond.** What will the group do about the issue in light of what they have learned from their own experiences set alongside the faith story? At this point, the faith story becomes lived rather than a mere intellectual exercise.

LOOK AHEAD

Here are reminders for what you need to do for the next session or two.

INSIGHTS FROM SCRIPTURE

Here is a resource for Explore the Bible. Don't try to use all the material given. Take what you need to lead the session and answer questions your group may have. Let the Insights section inspire you to think and study more about the passage for the session.

›› HANDOUT SHEETS

Occasionally, there will be a handout sheet to complement your session. If you choose to use this, you will need to make enough copies for the group. These sheets may include questions, stories, agree/disagree exercises, charts, pictures, and other materials to stimulate your group to think and discuss.

Generally, no participant preparation is required unless the session plan calls for you to contact selected group members for specific tasks.

>>> **SESSION 1**

YOUR BASIC 'WAY OUT' GOD >>>

>>> KEY VERSE

"The Lord is my strength and my might, and he has become my salvation; this is my God, and I will praise him, my father's God, and I will exalt him." (Exodus 15:2)

>>> FAITH STORY

Exodus 15:1-21

>>> FAITH FOCUS

Having experienced the drama of being saved from the Egyptian army, both Moses and Miriam sang songs of praise to God. Their two songs shout out the story of God's saving grace, of God's liberation. They highlight a basic tenet of our faith—that God is a liberator, one who provides *a way out*. For Jews and Christians alike, this event of liberation is a pinnacle in the story of faith (salvation history). It is an event not just of the past, but one that accompanies the faithful throughout life.

>>> SESSION GOAL

For participants who sometimes wonder whether or not God is involved in human history, introduce them to this turning point in salvation history—the exodus.

>>> Materials needed and advance preparation

- Chalkboard/chalk or newsprint/markers
- Twister games, or children's large cardboard blocks, large cardboard appliance box and tape (depending on option you choose in Focus)
- Index cards, pencils
- Bibles
- Copies of handout sheet for Session 1
- Hoses and water source (option in Respond)

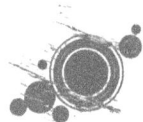

TEACHING PLAN

1. FOCUS 10 minutes

>>> **Option A:** If you can get your hands on a large cardboard appliance box, use it to box up one or more of your participants. Provide tape to tape it shut. Other possibilities include building a tower around a person out of children's large cardboard blocks (from your church nursery?) so that the person inside is "stuck" unless they break down the wall. You could also lock one or more youth in a closet for about 10 minutes (though be careful of very real fears this may expose). The idea is to let youth feel, even momentarily, as if they're stuck without a way out.

DOING DRUGS AS A WAY OUT...

Peer pressure got the kids doing drugs? Not really, reports Knight-Ridder News Service. It's more likely that kids who do drugs are trying to find a way out of their problems, to escape. Plus, they just like the feeling. What youth don't yet understand is that in the long run drugs pose obstacles to developing problem-solving skills.

> "The God celebrated [in the songs of Moses and Miriam] is not an abstract God, an idea, however lofty. This God is known because the action can be recognized in specific events."
>
> Etienne Charpentier, *How to Read the Old Testament*

>> **Option B:** Play Twister to achieve the same purpose: Let participants feel, even momentarily, as if they're stuck without a way out (except if they fall). Depending on the size of your group, have multiple games going. Let the adults have fun, too, but playing their own game!

2. CONNECT 5-8 minutes

As a group, tell stories of scary times when you were (literally or figuratively) locked up, locked out, tied up, boxed in, twisted up, and couldn't find a way out.

Discuss in small groups of 2-4 people (write the questions on the chalkboard or newsprint):

1. How do you feel when you can't get out of a place or a situation?
2. What do you do; kick, scream, yell, pray, run, something worse?
3. Where do you think God is when you're scared and can't find a way out?

Shift to the next activity by saying: *Most likely we've all felt stuck or locked up, with no way out. We've wondered where God was. That's how the Israelites must have felt as slaves. Then something happened, something they would remember as long as there were storytellers.*

3. EXPLORE THE BIBLE 10-12 minutes

Briefly recap the story of the exodus: how Moses got Pharaoh to let the people go, how the slaves fled before the Egyptian army, how they came to the banks of the Red Sea and God provided dry ground for the crossing, how the waters rolled back over the army, drowning the Egyptians.

Invite participants to read Exodus 15:1-21 *aloud*. The victory songs are better that way! Essentially, there are two choruses responding to each other (you could even divide in two and do it that way—antiphonally). One is about the power of God in general (vv. 2-3, 6-7, 11, 18), and the other one celebrates specific acts of God (vv. 1, 4-5, 8-10, 12-17). Then choose one of the following options:

>> **Option A:** Rewrite the song of Moses (vv. 1b-18) into a rap. Don't try to get all the biblical facts and images into the rap, but use the story as a launching pad. If participants are not into rap, try developing a country and western song, or a blues style. If singing is not your group's "thing," develop a dramatic reading or one-act play.

>> **Option B:** Distribute copies of the handout sheet for a Bible study on how God helped the Israelites find a way through their post-escape problems.

>> **For Both Options:** If participants question the "warrior God" imagery in these passages, point out that this may be seen as symbolic language; "speaking of the warrior is a way of saying that, 'God is not distant; [God] is not absent from human struggles for justice and liberty'" (Etienne Charpentier).

Also, if you have time, help participants answer these questions (also taken from Charpentier):

- *What specific actions of God are celebrated in vv. 4-5 and 8-10?*
- *At this period it was thought that God had a precise purpose in liberating the Israelites (v. 17): what was it?*
- *What does v. 18 teach us about the faith of Israel and its political system?*

4. APPLY 5-10 minutes

Say something like: *In the song of Moses, God provides a way out—God parts the waters of the Red Sea and the people of Israel cross over to a safe place on dry ground. That does not mean that God makes the "other side" perfect. It means you get to keep going.*

At this point, tell the following story:

Basil Marin was pastor of Family Mennonite Church, a congregation in south-central Los Angeles. One night as Pastor Basil returned to his home from a meeting, he was hit in a head-on collision by a car driven by a person fleeing a high-speed police pursuit. The accident investigators estimate Pastor Basil's car was struck at about 90 mph.

Mistaken for the subject of the pursuit, Pastor Basil awoke to a gun barrel of a Los Angeles police officer's service revolver pressed into his ear. In the collision, Pastor Basil sustained serious injury. Nevertheless, the police handcuffed Pastor Basil and made him lie face down, on a broken nose, in the highway, until they discovered his Bible on the front seat of the car with his name on the cover. Only then did the police summon an ambulance and transport him to a hospital, where Pastor Basil spent two weeks recovering from the worst of his injuries. After the incident, Pastor Basil sought reconciliation with the officers who mistook him for the subject of their chase. The police refused to meet with him. Later, Pastor Basil said that it was his belief that God was with him during the accident, and that God never abandoned him, that has kept him from hating the police.

Ask: *How did Pastor Basil get out of his predicament? What do you think God's role was in providing a way out?*

5. RESPOND 10-15 minutes

Ask each participant to take an index card, and write on the card one area in their life where they would want God to provide a way out. Then rearrange the chairs in your meeting place so that you have two rows of chairs with an aisle between the rows. Invite each participant to walk between the chairs, placing their cards in a box, symbolizing that they are willing to walk between the waters of their crisis and disappointment and trust God to provide a way through their situation, and onward, maybe not to a perfect resolution, but always to a fresh start.

```
x x x x x x x x x
o ————————> box
x x x x x x x x x
```

Note: In a camp or retreat setting, or if you can do this activity outside, have participants walk between a couple of people with hoses, who arc the water over their heads, symbolizing the waters of the sea through which the Israelites passed.

Close with a prayer thanking God for providing a way out, and asking God to give each participant courage to walk through their fears and crises to God's way through.

> "The God of Exodus is the God of history and of political liberation..."
>
> Gustavo Gutiérrez,
> *A Theology of Liberation*

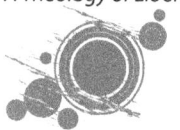

LOOK AHEAD

For next session, one of the activity options requires one deck of cards (Uno, Rook, or Dutch Blitz) for every four people. Another calls for a tent. You may also want to make a poster on newsprint of the Ten Commandments, as a refresher for your participants.

If you plan to do the Extender Session option of a Seder or Haggadah service, collect your resources (see sources listed in Extender) so you can have the service following this or the next session.

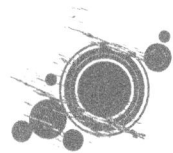

>>>
Winston Churchill, the British Prime Minister during World War II, was quoted as saying, "Success is never final. Failure is never fatal. It is the courage to continue that counts."

 # INSIGHTS FROM SCRIPTURE

Exodus 15:1-21 is part of a larger unit (Exodus 13:17–18:27) that describes the perils of the initial passage to freedom for Israel. They departed Egypt, journeyed to Mt. Sinai, and there entered into a covenant with God. Coping with the ongoing crises associated with leaving Egypt is the central theme of this section. In each story, Moses and the people of Israel are inadequate to meet the challenges of their newfound freedom. God had embraced the Israelites when they were a people in bondage, then proved to be an active, dynamic, and interested participant as they met each crisis. God parted the waters (14:19-30), provided fresh water (15:22-27; 17:5-6), fed them with manna (16:14-15), gave Aaron and Hur the idea of lifting Moses' arms up over the battle with the Amalekites (17:8-13), and gave Jethro the wisdom to suggest Moses could not run the entire operation of moving God's people to the Promised Land by himself (18:19-27).

Exodus 15:1-21 is a pair of Hebrew songs that celebrate God's involvement and reliability in dangerous times. There are two songs in the text; vv. 1b-18 is Moses' song, made up of a chorus (v. 1b) and six couplets (vv. 2-18); v. 19 is a transitional narrative statement; vv. 20-21 describe the song of Miriam and the women, which is Moses' chorus (cf. v. 21).

>> WHAT ABOUT THE BLOOD?

Participants may see the Hebrew Bible as a difficult and confusing collection of materials. Our churches preach peace, yet in Exodus 15, a whole army gets slaughtered. But there is a rabbinical story (*midrash*) of Exodus 15 that describes Moses celebrating the victory over Egypt, only to discover God crying over the destruction of the Egyptians. This story is not primarily about "beating the bad guys." It is a reminder that God takes the initiative to save people, and cautions the reader from becoming too arrogant and self-reliant. That Moses and the people of Israel seemed to fail at every turn is not to suggest they are somehow stupid. Life is full of failures. Exodus 15 is a celebration of God's ongoing journey with us, as we move in life away from all that enslaves us, toward the freedom (albeit costly) offered in Jesus Christ.

Even the locale of this event of liberation is significant to the story. Bodies of water, like the Red Sea, served in the Hebrew Scriptures as symbols of chaos. The people of Israel had to journey through the midst of chaos to get to a new start. Often, the only way available to us in the middle of our disappointments is to rely on God for a way out when everything is chaos, and recognize that life is not about avoiding chaos, but having God as a companion on the journey when chaos is at hand.

>> THE WAY OUT

The message of the exodus is that God provides a way out. *Ex houdos* comes from the Greek meaning "out way," the way out. In other words, the entire Bible is about *another way*. When the infant Jesus' life was in danger, his parents took him "another way" to escape Herod (Matthew 2). The magi went home "another way." Then Jesus started teaching "another way." The early church was known as The Way. A basic tenet of both Jewish and Christian faith is that God is a liberator, *one who provides a way*.

YOUR BASIC 'WAY OUT' GOD

The people of Israel were en route from slavery in Egypt to freedom in the Promised Land when the Egyptian army tried to recapture them and return them to slavery. God rescued Moses and the people by parting the Red Sea, thus providing an escape for Israel, which Moses and Miriam sing about in Exodus 15:1-21. Yet after the escape, the road to freedom wasn't any easier. Using the chart below, examine a few of the situations the people of Israel faced after they were freed, and how God worked to help them find a way through their problems.

Text	Problem	The Way Out
Exodus 14:1-31	Egyptian army attempts to recapture Israel	God parts the Red Sea, allowing Israel to escape
Exodus 15:22-27		
Exodus 16:1-36		
Exodus 17:1-7		
Exodus 17:8-16		
Exodus 18:13-27		

Permission is granted to photocopy this handout for use with this session.

>>> SESSION 2

YOUR BASIC COVENANT >>>

>>> KEY VERSES

"I am the Lord your God, who brought you out of the land of Egypt, out of the house of slavery; you shall have no other gods before me." (Exodus 20:2-3)

>>> FAITH STORY

Exodus 20:1-17

>>> FAITH FOCUS

God gave a set of summary commandments to establish boundaries and goals for positive living. God initiated this covenant to bring about right relationship between God and the people. To establish the covenant, however, God needs a response from the people. It can't be a forced, one-way relationship. Basic to Jewish and Christian faith is the notion of covenant, the heart of which is represented by these "ten words" of God.

>>> SESSION GOAL

As youth are acquiring values, invite them to order their lives around these ten words of covenant, as a response to God's faithfulness.

>>> Materials needed and advance preparation

- One deck of cards (Uno, Rook, or Dutch Blitz) for every four people
- Handout sheets for Session 2
- Bible dictionaries and concordances, one set for every two people, if possible
- Newsprint and markers
- Writing paper, pencils
- Tent (option in Apply)
- Prepare a list of things you are willing to do, or covenant, as youth leader or Sunday school leader (*Option A* in Respond).
- Candles, cups, grape juice or sparkling juice for wine, and challah (a special egg bread) for Shabbat service (*Option B* in Respond)

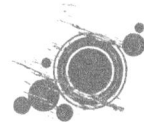

TEACHING PLAN

1. FOCUS 10-15 minutes

>>> **Option A** (*for groups who want to study the covenant of the Ten Commandments in specific*):

Divide into groups of four (one group is fine) and ask them to play several hands of cards. As you divide the groups up, designate one of the participants (in secret) not to play by the rules (e.g., doesn't play the correct suit in a game of Rook). IT IS VERY IMPORTANT THE OTHER PARTICIPANTS DO NOT KNOW THAT ONE PERSON WILL NOT BE PLAYING BY THE RULES.

Continue with *Option A* under Connect.

>> **Option B** (*for groups who want to study the more overarching theme of covenant*):

Roommates' agreement: Pair participants up, one boy and one girl in each pair if possible (for a mock prenuptial agreement). If this gender pairing doesn't work for your group, have participants pair up *to hammer out an agreement as if they were to be roommates for at least ten years*. You could also invite them to work in threes, which could make the activity even more interesting! Remind them that they have to stay together at least ten years (longer in the case of the "prenuptial" agreement!), so they can't just move out if the going gets tough. Have them focus on these questions as they work out an agreement (add some of your own):

- How will you share the costs of groceries? Who will make up the list? What if one person eats more than the other?
- How will you handle paying previous debts (car loans, school loans, etc.)?
- How will you decide where to live? What if you need to move?
- How will you decide if or where you'll go to church?
- Will you keep a budget? What will happen if someone goes over?
- How will you agree on guests at your place? What if one of you likes to party loudly and the other wants private space?
- Is there any danger you'll run into the "odd couple" syndrome, one of you a slob and one a neat freak?
- What about pets? What if someone is allergic?
- (Other issues that come up...) Continue with *Option B* under Connect.

2. CONNECT 5-8 minutes

>> **Option A:** Discuss what it was like to try to play the card game when one person was not playing by the rules.

Shift to the next activity by saying: *Without rules we'd probably have chaos, right? Here are some rules that are really basic to us as people of God.*

Go on to Explore...

>> **Option B:** Share some of the agreements, then ask questions such as, What was the best thing about working out a prenuptial (or roommate) agreement? The worst thing? What was the easiest thing? The hardest thing? Was it easier to agree on broad issues or on the little things? Could you agree on which were the *big* things and which were *little*? Did you frame agreements in terms of things you *will* do or things you *won't* do? Why? Ask for a show of hands of those who believe they'd be able to keep *their* part of the agreement. Why? Did you make provisions for if the agreement gets broken?

Shift to the next activity by saying: *If you ended up with a lot of do's and don'ts in your agreement, you may look back sometime and wonder why you made all those rules. But what you know deep down is that it's only by keeping the agreement that you keep the relationship alive. God knows that too, of course.*

Go on to Explore...

3. **EXPLORE THE BIBLE** 15-20 minutes

Choose either or both of the following:

- Ask three participants to do the Reader's Theater (on the "Hammer It Out" handout sheet), taken from Exodus 20:1-17.
- Read each of the Ten Commandments, from Exodus 20:1-7 (found on second handout sheet). Follow each Bible reading with the corresponding "beatitude" (also found on handout sheet).

Now do a word study of *covenant* as it's used in the Bible. This will give your group practice using a Bible dictionary and concordance. Provide these tools, one set for every two people, if possible. Your pastor or church library will likely have them, or you can search online.

Start by reading Joshua 24:16-18, 23-25, as an example of a way of renewing the covenant. Then have participants look up the word *covenant* in a Bible, theological dictionary, or online so they'll have an idea of what they're looking for when they move to the concordance. Then, look it up in a concordance, and note how many times it occurs in the Hebrew Bible, then in the New Testament. (See list at end of Insights for other references to covenant.) Point out that some even refer to the Old and New Testaments as the Old and New Covenants. Look up and read some of the references. Does covenant mean the same thing every time? Ask them to keep a chart of the different senses of meaning you find. In each passage, pay attention to who is making the covenant. Do the conditions of the covenant seem equal? How many other words can you come up with that mean pretty much the same thing as covenant (ex: pact, agreement, bond, treaty, promise, contract, deal, understanding, transaction, bargain). How do you think a covenant is *different* from these words?

4. **APPLY** 5-8 minutes

>> **Option A:** Discuss together the following questions:

*Does society today need rules like the Ten Commandments? Why? Are there any we **don't** really need anymore?*

Why do you think God made the Ten Commandments sound so negative ("You shall not...")? (Possible answers: framing them in negative leaves open all the other possibilities, even though they're "negative," God doesn't specify a punishment.)

- *If these "ten words" (which is also the meaning of Decalogue) are part of a covenant, why do you think we've come to call them commandments, since covenant is an agreement?*
- *What might be **missing** from the Ten Commandments that we need today?*
- *What are the consequences of **not** keeping a covenant?*

Summarize by supplying participants with the image of the "ten words" not as *rules*, but as *tent poles*, that provide structure to the tent that is the promise of God to give us a life that works, that shelters us. These ten poles hold up a tent, and that tent can increase our chances for survival in the wilderness. If we ignore them, it doesn't mean God's going to love us any less. But our chances for survival in this wilderness of life decrease.

>> **Option B:** On a large piece of newsprint, have participants develop their own commandments in the form of graffiti art. Use symbols, abbreviations, and short phrases to communicate, update, or even invent new commandments. Place this sheet of newsprint next to a posting of the "Ten Commandments" handout sheet. Ask participants to describe their graffiti, and the message behind their artwork.

> "Thus the Church of Christ acknowledges that, according to God's saving design, the beginnings of her faith and her election are found already among the Patriarchs, Moses, and the prophets... The Church, therefore, cannot forget that she received the revelation of the Old Testament through the people with whom God in His inexpressible mercy concluded the Ancient Covenant."

Declaration on the Relation of the Church to Non-Christian Religions, 2.

》》 **Option C:** Give participants the task of **setting up a tent**, but don't give them the poles or supports. (You can either set it up inside or outside, depending on the size of the tent.) When they complain about the impossibility of the task, give them the poles to complete the task. Then, if the tent is big enough, hold the rest of the session inside.

Discuss what it was like to try to set up the tent without the structural supports. Remind participants that the Israelites traveled in tents through the wilderness, and then suggest to them that the tent is like the promise that God will be with us on our journey, giving us shelter in the wilderness. But in order to be really effective, the promise needs some structure, like the tent needed the poles in order to be very helpful as a tent. The "ten words" that Moses brought to the people were not just a bunch of arbitrary rules, but *tent poles*, the structure for the "tent" that is the promise of God. When these ten poles hold up a tent, that tent can increase our chances for survival in the wilderness. If we ignore them, it doesn't mean God's going to love us any less. We've still got the tent. But our chances for survival in this wilderness of life decrease.

5. RESPOND 8-10 minutes

》》 **Option A:** Make your own covenant with each other. Come to the meeting with a list of things you are willing to do, or covenant, as youth leader or Sunday school leader. These may also be things you have done in the past to nurture the group. (Many covenants begin with a list of the things one party has already done for the other.)

Examples: I promise to...
- prepare for every time we meet.
- answer any calls or texts you make to me, and if I'm not availalbe, I'll get back to you.
- shave my head and let you auction me off at a fund-raiser.
- provide a ride if you need to get to church, or home, or get stuck somewhere.
- call or text (or other social media contact) once a week to see how you're doing.

Next, invite participants to make an individual or collective covenant *in response* to your part of the covenant. Given what you promised, what will *they* do? Keep the covenant!

Close with prayer, thanking God for loving us enough to provide a structure for living in the "ten words," and asking God to give you and your participants wisdom and energy to follow through on commitments.

》》 **Option B:** Keep the portion of the covenant outlined in the fourth commandment:

Remember the Sabbath. Invite a Jewish person to lead a Sabbath, or Shabbat, service for the group. Coordinate with this person in advance about what materials you will need to provide. You may need to supply candles, cups, wine or grape juice, and challah (a special egg bread). Use the prayers below, or create a different worship aid in coordination with the person who will be leading the service.

Observant Jews keep the Sabbath from sundown on Friday to sundown on Saturday every week, beginning and ending with Sabbath prayers. The handout outlines prayers and actions that take place just before the Friday evening meal is served.

Remember, this is a *Jewish* prayer, and part of their sacred tradition. It is important to take your lead from your Jewish guest as to how to go about this in a way that is respectful of their tradition.

Service for Shabbat

(Light candles.)

We kindle the lights of shabbat, seeing them as symbols of human enlightenment and human kindness. Let us remember the generations before us who lit candles as we do, and found beauty and serenity in their light. Together we kindle the lights of shabbat.
Na-eh ha-or ba-olam. Na-eh ha-or ba-shalom. Na-eh ha-or ba-shabbat.
How wonderful is the light of the world. How radiant are the candles of peace.
How beautiful are the lights of shabbat.

(Serve the wine substitute.)

Wine is the symbol of the wholeness of life. There are times when we drink from bitter cups, yet there are also times when we savor the sweetness and joy that exult life. Wine thus points to the recognition that life is both joy and sorrow. We resolve to accept them both and so affirm all of life. These provide the happiness of which this cup speaks. Let us raise our cups to the fullness that is life.
Na-eh shalom ba-olam. Na-eh shalom ba-adam. Na-eh shalom ba-shabbat.
How wonderful is peace in the world. How glorious is peace among all people. How beautiful is the peace of shabbat.

(All present drink.)

SONG : Hee-nay ma-tov u-ma-na-eem She-vet a-kheem gam ya-khad.
Behold how good it is when brothers and sisters dwell together in unity.

(Serve the challah.)

As the fingers of the challah intertwine, so do we join hands in our common humanity, sharing the fruits of our labor. We cherish all that has been created through human effort. We celebrate the accomplishments of yesterday and today, anticipating the possibilities of tomorrow. May the sharing of this challah strengthen our bonds with others who walk upon this earth.

Na-eh a-mal ka-pay-noo. Na-eh le-khem ha-aretz. Na-eem ha-mo-tsee-eem le-khem meen ha-a-rets.

How beautiful is the work of our hands.
How wonderful is the bread of the earth. How glorious are those who bring forth bread from the earth.

(All present eat challah.)

We honor the shabbat, a day of rest and peace. Throughout Jewish history, the observance of shabbat has served as a manifestation of human dignity. Shabbat is a gift we give ourselves—a gift of time to use as we wish. Let us celebrate together the end of another week in the company of friends and family.

SONG: Shalom kha-vay-reem, shalom kha-vay-reem, Shalom, shalom! L'-heet ra-ot, l'-heet ra-ot,
Shalom, shalom!
Peace to our friends
Until we meet again.
Peace.
Shabbat shalom!

LOOK AHEAD

For the next session on salvation, you'll need a large, thick blanket, and scraps of light-colored cloth.

Participants will use these scraps to write on, so you'll also need fine-point markers.

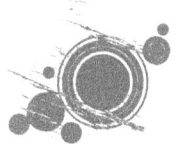

>>>
Imagine this scene from the comic strip "Non Sequitur":

Moses is holding the two tablets on a hill, looking down at the people below, saying, "Hmmm. Good question. I'll go back and find out." He trudges all the way back up the mountain, you see the glow of the bush behind the curve of the road, and he then reappears with his face all smoky. He says, "Yes, you have to obey all of them all of the time. And this concludes the %#@*%#@* question and answer period."

 # INSIGHTS FROM SCRIPTURE

Exodus 20:1-17 is a summary of the covenantal relationship God sought with Israel, a covenant intended to bring about right relationship between God and the people. It is more comprehensive than other such summaries (see Exodus 34, or Leviticus 19, as examples). As George Pixley says, "They [the commandments] constitute [God's] solemn declaration of the conditions for membership [in the people of God]" (from *On Exodus*, by George Pixley).

Here is how Israel likely understood this covenant and responded to it in daily life. First, the people understood the commandments as having two basic themes: reverence for God; and respect for people (though in ancient Israel any offense was considered an affront against God).

Reverence for God
1. No foreign gods
2. No images (of God)
3. Do not misuse God's name
4. Remember the sabbath

Respect for People
5. Honor father and mother
6. Do not kill
7. Do not commit adultery
8. Do not steal
9. Do not bear false witness
10. Do not covet

Second, the "ten words" that Moses brought to the people were not just a bunch of arbitrary rules, but life principles, or *tent poles* to give structure to the "tent" that is the promise of God. That promise is to give us a life that works. When these ten poles hold up a tent, that tent can increase our chances for survival in the wilderness. If we ignore them, it doesn't mean God's going to love us any less. We've still got the tent. But our chances for survival in this wilderness of life decrease.

Third, while the "ten words" sometimes get a bad rap for their negative tone ("thou shalt not..."), it is important to realize that they could not be framed in any other way. They were designed to define a standard of ethical behavior, to set limits. The ten words (decalogue: deca = ten, logue = word) lay out major principles on which God based a relationship with Israel. So if the tone is negative, think of all that one *can* do! Also notice that God sets these conditions, but in a rare turn does not list punishments if they are broken. Certainly there are consequences. But God is not poised to snatch away the promise at the least infraction of the rules. If that were the case, God would never have bothered, since the commandments were already being broken even as Moses trudged down Sinai weighted with the gift of words. The people were already dancing around an image of their own making, and they *still* got the gift of the Law, a structure for their journey with God.

>> WHAT IS A COVENANT?

The Ten Commandments are an integral part of the key to the relationship between God and the Israelites: the concept of covenant. The Hebrew term b^erit, which we would translate "covenant," appears 287 times in the Hebrew Bible. Covenants were, in the ancient Near East, "made" between two parties, in which the greater committed themselves to the lesser in the context of mutual loyalty. Sometimes there was even a freewill granting of privileges. What was unique about this covenant was that a *God* would stoop to be one of the parties.

Covenants followed a certain prescribed pattern. Below is a sample of the pattern of the covenant of the ancient Near East, using Exodus 20:1-17 as a guide:

> Beginning: "I am the Lord your God...." v. 2a
> Reminder: "who brought you out of the land of Egypt" v. 2b
> Obligations: The "ten words," vv. 3-17

In later Jewish study of the scriptures it has been noted that the events of the book of Exodus, including the giving of the covenant on Sinai, follow the pattern of a courtship and marriage—rescue, courting, wedding with stipulations, home planning, infidelity, reconciliation, and the final "moving in" (to Canaan) (Everett Fox, *The Five Books of Moses*). Thus the Ten Commandments are not some abstract philosophical set of rules, but the basis for how Israel responded to God's grace and deliverance from Egypt.

Israel repeatedly tested the covenant, thereby testing the relationship with God. The formula of covenant is clearly repeated in Joshua 24. There is a lengthy recounting of all the ways God kept the covenant (Josh. 24:1-13), and then a repeated invitation to the people to respond to God's grace (Josh. 24:14, 19-20). Even though the terms themselves of the covenant are not equal in the responsibilities of each party, it is nevertheless mutual in that a response is required from the "lesser" party. Joshua exemplified a way to renew covenant.

Baptism, too, is a sign of covenant that establishes the "lesser" party's acceptance of the conditions of the covenant. Just as the Israelites agreed to be God's people as they received the commandments on Sinai, so baptism symbolizes our willingness to be disciples of Jesus, and to join the body of believers, God's people. Thus the notion of covenant marches its unifying theme through the ages of the Christian church.

God created people for relationship. For a relationship to occur, the parties involved must agree on some sort of scope of the relationship. That is covenant, basic to a faith relationship with God.

> "The commands are best understood when kept in closest relation to the God of the covenant who laid claim upon a people and pointed them to a new life as the people of God."
>
> Brevard Childs, *Exodus*

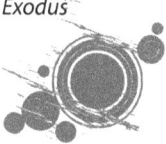

OLD AND NEW COVENANTS

Gen. 21:27, 32
1 Sam. 18:3; 23:18
1 Kings 20:34
Gen. 2:16, 17
Gen. 6:18
Gen. 9:12, 15, 16
Gen. 13:17; 15:18; 17:2, 4, 7, 11, 13, 14, 19
2 Kings 13:23
1 Chron. 16:15-18
Ps. 105:9-11
Acts 7:8
Rom. 4:13, 17
Ex. 31:16
Deut. 4:13, 23
Jer. 31:31-34
Heb. 8:8-11
John 7:39
Acts 2:32, 33
2 Cor. 3:6-9
Acts 10:44-47
Heb. 10:15-17

Exploring tough questions facing youth today

Well, the time has finally come. You're about to go out into the big wide world on your own. Only trouble is, the big wide world is a little pricey. In order to make it, you'll have to share a place to live, and that means getting a roommate or . . . getting married! In order to minimize the hassles, you decide to start off with an agreement about the living situation.

So pair up to *hammer out an agreement as if you were to be roommates for at least ten years*. (You could really save money if you'd do it as a threesome, but you'd have to decide if you could lead such an "interesting" life!) Remember, you have to stay together at least ten years (longer in the case of the "prenuptial" agreement!). Focus on these questions as you work out an agreement:

- How will you share the costs of groceries? Who will make up the list? What if one person eats more than the other?
- How will you handle paying previous debts (car loans, school loans, etc.)?
- How will you decide where to live? What if you need to move?
- How will you decide if or where you'll go to church?
- Will you keep a budget? What will happen if someone goes over?
- How will you agree on guests at your place? What if one of you likes to party loudly and the other wants private space?
- Is there any danger you'll run into the "odd couple" syndrome, one of you a slob and one a neat freak?
- What about pets? What if someone is allergic?
- (Other issues that come up . . .)

THE TEN WORDS READER'S THEATER PRESENTS:

Reader 1: God spoke to the people, saying—

Reader 2: I am Yahweh, your God. I brought you out of slavery.

Reader 3: Worship me alone.

Reader 1: Do not attempt to picture me as any living creature. You will only end up worshiping your creation instead of me. I want you to struggle with the Mystery that "I am."

Reader 2: Respect my Name. Do not abuse my Name by associating it with lies and angry curses.

Reader 3: Work hard for six days, then take the seventh day off. I did it, and I liked it. Stop working and remember that you are more than what you **do**.

Reader 1: Respect your parents, as you respect my name. If you do, things will go well for you.

Reader 2: Don't kill. Period.

Reader 3: Don't mess around with marriage vows, yours or anyone else's. Period.

Reader 1: Don't steal. Period.

Reader 2: Tell the truth, to and about your neighbors.

Reader 3: Some people are always going to have some stuff that is better than yours. Don't waste your time trying to figure out how to get better stuff.

Permission is granted to photocopy this handout for use with this session.

The Ten Commandments

(from Exodus 20:1-17 NRSV)

1. You shall have no other gods before me.
2. You shall not make for yourself an idol.
3. You shall not make wrongful use of the name of the Lord your God.
4. Remember the sabbath day and keep it holy.
5. Honor your father and your mother.
6. You shall not murder.
7. You shall not commit adultery.
8. You shall not steal.
9. You shall not bear false witness against your neighbor.
10. You shall not covet.

The Beatitudes

(from Matthew 5:3-11)

Blessed are the poor in spirit, for theirs is the kingdom of heaven.

Blessed are those who mourn, for they will be comforted.

Blessed are the meek, for they will inherit the earth.

Blessed are those who hunger and thirst for righteousness, for they will be filled.

Blessed are the merciful, for they will receive mercy.

Blessed are the pure in heart, for they will see God.

Blessed are the peacemakers, for they will be called children of God.

Blessed are those who are persecuted for righteousness' sake, for theirs is the kingdom of heaven.

Blessed are you when people revile you and persecute you and utter all kinds of evil against you falsely on my account. Rejoice and be glad, for your reward is great in heaven, for in the same way they persecuted the prophets who were before you.

Permission is granted to photocopy this handout for use with this session.

>>> **SESSION 3**

YOUR BASIC SALVATION >>>

>>> KEY VERSES

"But so that you may know that the Son of Man has authority on earth to forgive sins"—he said to the paralytic—"I say to you, stand up, take your mat and go to your home." (Mark 2:10-11)

>>> FAITH STORY

Mark 2:1-12

>>> FAITH FOCUS

When people began realizing that Jesus had something to relieve their sufferings, they followed him in droves. Jesus wasn't just healing bodies, however, but also souls. How? By forgiving sins. Jesus offers us the hope of salvation by accepting us as we are, and inviting us to healing and wholeness by connecting to his way of sacrificial love.

>>> SESSION GOAL

Challenge participants to accept Jesus' unconditional offer of healing and hope, which is salvation.

>>> Materials needed and advance preparation

- Thick blanket
- Writing paper, pencils
- Scraps of light-colored cloth and fine-point markers (see Apply)
- Bibles

TEACHING PLAN

1. FOCUS 5 minutes

Draft two people to hold up a thick blanket between you and the rest of the group, like a curtain. Tell the group to imagine that this "curtain" extends to infinity to both sides, as well as above and below you. They can't touch it, get over it, go around it, or pass through it. Now ask the group to try to *show they love you* (hugs, looks, words, etc.). With the blanket in the way, it will be tricky to do. You can't show love to them either.

2. CONNECT 5 minutes

Now take the blanket/curtain away. Let participants try their expressions of love on you now, and you show them, too. Discuss how it is to be able to show and receive expressions of love without the blanket in the way.

In Real Life | Testing the Waters   25

Then explain that the blanket symbolizes everything that gets in the way between us and God, all the things we do that make it hard to get close to God, to love God. We call that sin, the things that get between us and God. That's why Jesus came. He taught us the way to live, and then he took away that curtain (an event we celebrate at Easter), and that made it possible for us to get close to God—if we choose.

Shift to the next activity by saying: *It's hard to get close to somebody when there's something separating us from them. The obvious solution is to get rid of the separation. That's what made some friends of a paralyzed guy dig a hole in a roof.*

IS CHURCH...

- a way for people to "commit" a sin, go to confession, get forgiven, and go out to sin all over again?
- a way to brainwash people into thinking if you "pray," everything good will happen to you?
- a place for people who can't think for themselves?
- where people with "wrong" beliefs are looked upon as subhuman?

3. EXPLORE THE BIBLE 15-20 minutes

Spend a few moments reading Mark 2:1-12 together. Create an improvisational theater piece based on the passage. The purpose is to tell the story from your own point of view.

First you will need to build the set. So have them build a "house" right in your room out of what you have available—small tables, couch cushions, the blanket you brought for Focus, etc.

Then you'll need the following characters:

- Jesus
- The paralyzed person
- Some friends (at least four, if possible)
- Members of the crowd, gathered to listen to Jesus

Retell the story, but don't worry about "doing it just right." Enjoy the process with the participants.

One way to put the improvisational piece together might be:

Begin with "Jesus" reading from another part of the Gospels, while the "crowd" asks him questions. At one point, a "friend" (of the paralytic) has a realization that Jesus could heal his friend. He slaps his head (a Simpson "duh!") and runs to where the paralytic and other friends are gathered. They put the paralyzed person on a sleeping bag (or a wheelchair?), and bring him/her to Jesus. How will they get rid of the "separation" (the "roof" of the set house) between their friend and Jesus? Finish up with a conversation like the one recorded in vv. 5-12.

Once you have acted the scene out, discuss together the following questions:

1. *What did it feel like to be your character?*
2. *How did your character react to the other characters? How did the crowd react to the friends of the paralyzed person? How did Jesus react to the paralyzed person?*
3. *Why do you think Jesus forgave the sins of the paralyzed person, and then healed the person?*

Next, take Bibles again and read Matthew 27:45-51, the story of Jesus' death and how the veil of the temple was torn in two. Explain that the veil was a heavy curtain behind which was the "holy of holies," which only priests who had been specially consecrated could approach. Suggest to them that, like lowering the blanket earlier in the session, the tearing of the veil symbolized the tearing away of that which separated "ordinary" people from God.

4. APPLY 5-8 minutes

Distribute scraps of light-colored cloth and fine-point markers. Invite participants to write things on the scrap that keep them from being the best person they can be, or things they believe separate them from God. You could ask, *What are the curtains that separate you and God?*

After giving some time to think and write, have them tear or cut their scraps in half to remind them that Jesus died to tear up those things that separate them from God.

5. RESPOND 10 minutes

Divide into pairs or threes, distribute paper and pencils. Invite participants to think of anyone they know, or even have only heard about, who is struggling with some problem or illness or relationship. List that problem, but don't use any names or identifying characteristics. They *may not* list themselves or their own problems in any way this time. Tell them they'll be trying to see which small group can come up with the *longest* list.

The point is to get them thinking about everyone *but* themselves. If Jesus saves us *from* whatever separates us from God, then he also saves us to be a people for others. That starts with practicing thinking of others.

When all the lists are tallied, have each small group circle one or two things on their list. These circled items will be part of the closing prayer. Close the session by praying for some of the concerns participants listed. After the prayer, tack the lists on the wall as a reminder to continue praying for those concerns of others.

LOOK AHEAD

For the next session on baptism, consider having the session by a creek, river, by the baptismal font, or by a wading pool. One of the Focus options includes inviting someone to be interviewed about their baptism; contact them now. Depending on the Apply option you choose, you'll need to photocopy songs about baptism from your song book, one set per every 3-4 participants.

INSIGHTS FROM SCRIPTURE

Have you ever heard of someone being rescued from the brink of death—drowning, burning, a cave-in—by a selfless hero who ended up dying instead? It's the Christ story, isn't it? Jesus gave up his own life to save all the rest of us who were flailing in our lives. But this very basic element of faith that we call salvation is not an easy concept to explain. What does salvation *mean*? From what are we saved? *To* what are we saved?

So here is a very short course on the meaning of salvation.

>> SINS ARE FORGIVEN

When people began realizing that Jesus had something to relieve their sufferings, they began following him in droves (Mark 2:1-12). Jesus wasn't "just" healing bodies, however, but also souls. How? By forgiving sins.

If you've ever deeply offended or hurt someone, you may also know the relief you feel if that person says, "It's okay. I still want to be with you. Thank you for apologizing." It means a burden is lifted, and you can concentrate on other things. You are, in essence, saved from having to dwell on that problem, and can go on to other activities. Salvation means sins are forgiven, and Jesus has authority to do it (Mark 2:1-12). Jesus can heal both body and soul, and we can get on with the business of being disciples.

>> ACCESS TO GOD'S GRACE

When Jesus died on the cross, scripture says the veil of the temple was torn in two, symbolizing that everyone would have access to God, who created us, loves us, and wants to be in relationship with us. We have access to God's grace because of Jesus (Romans 5:1-5). Being saved means being in a right relationship with God, a *living* relationship, not a frozen moment in time. We aren't necessarily saved from *suffering*, but we have the Holy Spirit, the "encourager," to enliven us.

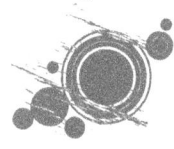

The friends of the paralyzed man went to all lengths to get their friend to healing, even breaking through the barrier of the roof that separated them from Jesus. In a similar way, Jesus went to all lengths, even dying, to break through the separation between us and God.

THE POWER OF DEATH IS BROKEN

Jesus shared our humanity, so that his death and resurrection wouldn't be just a trick by some God, but a real defeat of the *power* of death over us (Hebrews 2:4-5). We don't have to be so *afraid* of death anymore, because we know that even death can't separate us from God's love.

> *O Love, how deep, how broad, how high!*
> *It fills the heart with ecstasy*
> *that God, the Son of God, should take our mortal form for mortals' sake.*

This hymn attributed to Thomas à Kempis, who lived in the 15th century, mirrors the apostle Paul's own Christ hymn of Philippians 2. God became proactive in history in a great new way by becoming subject to the human condition. What does a God-in-the-flesh look like? It looks like Jesus, a person who responded to God most creatively, absolutely, and with the most discipline and faith. For the Christian, Jesus was God's most intensive embodiment. But God is still among us, and thus other people have been filled with God and responded creatively, and with discipline and faith. Jesus saved us by showing us how to be a person for others, and the Holy Spirit gives us the energy to be that person for others.

SOMEONE TO TURN TO

In Christ, God stands ready to forgive us, heal us, and befriend us. In Christ, God has acted in a unique way to reach out past our self-imposed barriers to meet us where we are. While we were paralyzed by sin and brokenness, God in Christ became our friend. This level of commitment was so strong, that even when the religious leaders plotted to kill him, Jesus remained committed even to them.

Commitment is like that. Jesus taught us the way to live, and then he took away the curtain (separation), an event we celebrate at Easter, and made it possible for us to get close to God—if we choose. Even though we often devise our own separations (sin), the invitation to healing and wholeness remains. Jesus offers us the hope of salvation in the form of a friendship based on our desire to be whole, and healing of our lives.

Jesus healed people from all kinds of sin, and from all kinds of disease, saving them to be people not just for themselves, but for others.

So salvation means sins are forgiven, we have access to God, and Jesus broke the power of fear that death instills in us. We are saved *from* whatever separates us from God (a.k.a. sin), including death, and we are saved to be a person for others.

> **"The whole of salvation history is the story of God looking for us: he offers us love and welcomes us with tenderness."**
>
> Pope Francis

SESSION 4

YOUR BASIC BAPTISM »»

»» KEY VERSE
So those who welcomed his message were baptized, and that day about three thousand persons were added. (Acts 2:41)

»» FAITH STORY
Acts 2:38-42

»» FAITH FOCUS
Peter's sermon on the day of Pentecost (Acts 2:14-40) ends with three thousand people getting baptized, a public welcoming of God's message of healing and hope in their lives. Baptism is a sign representing both God's faithfulness to the covenant with us and of our commitment to respond to that faithfulness. It's one of the basics of faith.

»» SESSION GOAL
Invite participants to consider the meaning of baptism as welcoming God's message into their lives, and being welcomed into the community of God's forgiven people.

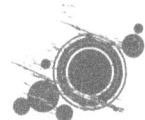

TEACHING PLAN

»» Materials needed and advance preparation
- Writing paper, pencils
- Bibles
- Chalkboard/chalk or newsprint/markers
- Make plans for getting the group to a creek, river, or the baptismal font for the session (see Focus).
- Invite your pastor, or an older person or couple to be interviewed about their baptism (*Option A* in Focus).
- Slips of paper with "tasks" (*Option B* in Focus)
- Copies of handout sheet for Session 4
- Photocopy songs about baptism from your song book, one set per every 3-4 participants (*Option A* in Apply)

1. FOCUS 10 minutes
Consider holding this entire session by a creek, river, lake, or by the baptismal font. The venue can make a big impact. If this is impossible, fill a baby wading pool and go outside in somebody's yard, or even just gather around a basin of water. Take along Bibles and song books, depending on the activity options you choose.

»» **Option A:** Invite someone from your parish who recently went through RCIA and was baptized. Alternatively, invite someone who recently became a godparent. Interview them about their baptism experience. Develop your own questions, or use some of these:

(for someone who went through RCIA and was baptized)
- *When and where were you baptized?*
- *Who performed your baptism?*

> "I don't think baptism is a giant step in our Christian walk with Christ, but it is an important first step. It is only the beginning. I didn't feel any different after I was baptized than before. (In fact, I choked as I was dunked in the water!) At first I was even a little let down because I wanted to feel like a change had come over my life…. I know I still question God and don't know exactly what I believe as far as my faith is concerned. I think God expects us to still question after we become a Christian, maybe even more than before because God can lead us in the right direction."
>
> Erin Mullins, student

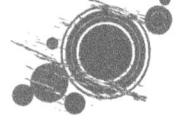

- *Why did you decide to be baptized?*
- *Did you have any special preparation or classes about the Christian faith before your baptism? Were you involved in any kind of special class or small group after your baptism?*
- *What did baptism mean to you when you were baptized? Has that meaning changed since your baptism? How?*
- *What advice would you give a younger person about baptism?*
- *How has baptism changed you and your relationship with God?*

(for someone who recently became a godparent)

- *What was your reaction when you were approached to be a godparent?*
- *Did you have any special preparation or classes about the Christian faith before the baptism? If yes, what did you learn in those classes?*
- *What personal meaning does being a godparent have for you? What special responsibilities do you have as a godparent?*
- *How does being a godparent affect your life as a follower of Jesus?*

Invite the interviewee(s) to stay and participate in the rest of the session.

Continue with *Option A* or *B* under Connect, deleting the first two sentences if you use *Option B*.

>> **Option B:** Explore an "initiation rite" to lead participants into thinking about baptism as a beginning of a life as part of the faith community. This activity will probably work best if you have chosen not to hold the session by a body of water. If you want to have it both ways, you'll need to adapt the tasks, below.

Make sure to arrive before any participants, and post yourself at the entrance to the meeting place. As each person arrives, hand them a slip of paper with a task on it (see below), and tell them they must perform this task in order to enter the room.

Tasks:
- Bring me a song book and three squares of toilet paper marking your favorite songs.
- Say the Lord's Prayer to me (if you can't, find someone who can).
- Bring me the most recent church bulletin *after* you have greeted anyone whose name is listed there. The person you greet must initial the bulletin.
- Bring six cups of cold water here for others to drink.
- Bring me one other person, and get them to turn around three times in front of me. Do this without speaking to them or me.

To match the number in your group, either make up more like these (notice they all have loose symbolism to things a baptized Christian might do), or duplicate them.

As each person accomplishes the task, give them a big hug and welcome them warmly.

Continue with *Option B* under Connect.

2. CONNECT 5-8 minutes

>> **Option A:** Distribute paper and pencils for each person. Ask them to write, in 25 words or less, their definition of church membership. Invite participants to share their definition with the entire group.

>> **Option B:** Ask, *How did it make you feel to have to do something to get in here?* Point out that it was sort of like an initiation rite. Have the group name some other "rites of passage"—special things we do to mark a significant event, turning point, or commitment to a person or program. Examples include driving (getting a license), getting married (exchanging rings). If you are inside, list these on the chalkboard or newsprint. If you are outside, just brainstorm.

Shift to the next activity by saying: *There are lots of reasons to express commitment. When we discover God's love for us through Jesus, we are baptized, as a symbol of our commitment to God and all of God's creation. Here's the story of a really big baptism.*

3. EXPLORE THE BIBLE 10-15 minutes

Acts chapter 2 is the story of the birth of the church. It was born by an act of the Holy Spirit and over 3,000 people were baptized to demonstrate their commitment to follow Jesus' Way and participate in the church.

Divide into small groups of no more than three or four (or do this activity individually). Make sure each person has access to a Bible. Invite participants to read Acts 2:29-47, and as a small group discuss together several questions. (Read them one at a time, or write them on the chalkboard or on newsprint.) Ask the person who has their birthday closest to the day of this session to record on a sheet of newsprint the findings of the group.

1. To what message did the 3,000 respond? (see vv. 29-36)
2. What happened after the baptism of the 3,000? (see vv. 42-47)
3. What do you like about this passage?
4. What questions do you have about this passage?
5. What does this passage say to you about your relationship with God?
6. What would you like to do differently as a result of this passage?

After about 5-6 minutes, return to the larger group for reporting. Discuss any questions that emerge from the passage, supplementing with information from the Insights from Scripture section.

Next, distribute handout sheets for participants to follow as you make the following points about the meaning of repentance and baptism. Use one or more participants as props:

- *Repentance is not just feeling sorry for sin; it is the conscious act of **turning away** from one's separation from God, accepting love and forgiveness, and **returning to** a right relationship with God* (turn participants around).
- *This right relationship with God is what the Bible means by "salvation." Salvation is a living relationship with God, not a moment frozen in time* (pretend to bop participants on the head, as if they've been "struck" by a moment of salvation).
- *Baptism expresses our readiness to repent, publicly confess our sin, receive forgiveness, and return to a right relationship with God (that is, experience salvation) through Jesus Christ.*
- *Baptism dramatizes our **dying** to the old life of sin (going under the water) and **rising** to the new life of membership and ministry within the body of Christ (coming up out of the water). It's also a symbol of the watery world of God's womb, from which comes new life.* (Have participants kneel and mime pushing them under the water or sprinkling, then help person rise again.)
- *Because baptism is the **beginning** of our Christian identity and discipleship, it requires genuine repentance and commitment, not moral perfection.*

>>>
"[You can consider baptism] as an act of birth in the watery tub . . . as a symbol for the womb of God. The Bible says we must be born from water and spirit, and the baptismal font can be like the waters of God's womb from which emerges new life. Of course it also stands for death, inasmuch as the old person is symbolically killed on the way down. And in a sense it is a reenactment of Jesus' death and resurrection."

Eric Vokel

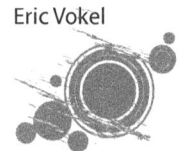

4. APPLY 8-10 minutes

>> **Option A: Match meanings of baptism with song phrases.** Photocopy baptism songs from your song book. Divide participants into groups of no more than three or four and pass out sets of the song sheets. Have participants mark phrases in each song where they find reference to one of the meanings of baptism on the handout sheet. Tell participants to number the baptism meanings so they have a little code.

>> **Option B:** Explore questions participants may have about infant versus adult baptisms in the Catholic tradition. Emphasize that *both are equally valid ways of welcoming someone into the community of faith.* Use the information presented in "Insights From Scripture" on the Catholic theology of baptism. Ask questions like:

- Who was baptized as an infant? Who hasn't been baptized yet?
- If you could choose, would you want to be baptized as an infant or as an adult? Why?
- What are the advantages of infant baptism? (The ritual emphasizes the gratuitousness of God's grace, since the infant clearly hasn't done anything to "earn" the grace of baptism; it welcomes a person into a loving, Christian community from the beginning of his or her life.)
- What are the advantages of waiting until you are an adult to be baptized? (You can make your own choice about faith; it is in line with the practice of the first Christians, as written down in the Bible.)
- [other questions you have about baptism...]

5. RESPOND 6-10 minutes

>> **Option A:** Ask participants to spend the next 3-4 minutes in quiet. Invite them to ask God if they are ready to indicate their willingness to take the next step of following Christ. For some, this may mean preparing to receive baptism (as well as confirmation and first Eucharist). More likely, it will mean preparing for confirmation in the Catholic Church. Make it clear that it takes great personal and spiritual courage to conclude that they may not be ready for baptism or confirmation, and that it's okay to admit they may not be ready. In the silence, pray silently for the Holy Spirit to call out participants who **are** ready for the step of baptism or confirmation. Invite those participants who feel like they would like to explore baptism or confirmation to set up a time to meet with you to discuss their desire.

Note: Find out in advance details of your parish confirmation programs as well as the protocol for preparing teens for baptism, so you can provide accurate information to youth about dates, times, meeting places, etc.

Close the session with a final prayer.

>> **Option B:** Distribute paper and pencils, and invite participants to write a very brief statement of faith that they might say *if* they were about to be baptized. Allow them to use Bibles, the handout sheet, or song books as resources. Some parishes invite all baptismal candidates to make such statements as part of the service of baptism. Have them answer: *If you were going to be baptized tomorrow, what would you say **today** in a faith statement to your parish? Why do you want to be baptized?* OR *What does being baptized mean to you now that you've expressed your commitment this way?*

Assure people that what they write today need only express their faith today. As they grow, their faith may shift and change. If you have some participants who clearly resist these questions, offer them opportunity to express reasons why they aren't ready to make a faith statement.

LOOK AHEAD

Session 5 asks you to prepare an edible snack that looks inedible (see Focus for a "recipe"), and hide small (but not too small) inedible "treasures" in it. Have some treasures to pass out at the end of the session. You will also need access to a sofa, and you may want to have a youth search out and bring some of the optional music listed for Respond.

If you will be using Extender *Option B* next session, make sure you have access to basins and towels for a footwashing service or its alternative.

 INSIGHTS FROM SCRIPTURE

Acts 2 is the story of the birth of the church. It takes place on the day of Pentecost, a Jewish harvest festival that happens some fifty days following Passover (these events took place in the same year when Jesus was killed during Passover). The text could be outlined in the following manner:

- vv. 1-4—The Holy Spirit comes upon the disciples.
- vv. 5-13—The disciples speak in other languages, and the crowd thinks they are drunk.
- vv. 14-36—Peter preaches a sermon from the book of Joel.
- vv. 37-41—The crowd responds to the sermon.
- vv. 42-47—A summary of the activity of the early church that emerged from this experience.

Verses 42-47 is a sort of report about the character and quality of life in the church. These "status reports" appear often in Acts (see 4:32-35; 6:7; 9:31; 12:24; 16:5; 19:20; 28:31). Each report reestablishes the major theme of the book of Acts: God's healing activity prevails, and the church grows.

The story of the growth of the church links conversion, baptism, and the life of discipleship into a single reality. Should we baptize at the end of a church membership class, or is the proper moment the beginning of a discipleship process? The answer in Acts seems to be, "yes." The early church saw conversion, baptism, and discipleship not as separate events, but as stages in the process of moving toward greater Christian maturity. Though Acts is the story of an ancient church, elements of its life are worth recovering for the 21st century. It can guide us on our faith journey, inviting us to make baptism an integral part of the whole conversion and discipleship process, and urging us to reclaim the Holy Spirit's presence and power for our time.

Baptism itself is a continuation of the story of God's intimate participation in the life of believers. That story began when Israel was born as a people, with the covenant that God made. Baptism, too, is a covenant. It means experiencing God's love and forgiveness, turning away from that which separates us from that love, and making a public commitment to be part of the community of believers.

BAPTISM IN THE CATHOLIC CHURCH

- The sacrament of baptism has evolved over the last 2,000 years. A good way to think of it now is as a **doorway into the body of Christ (the church)** and as a **public marker** of someone's commitment to follow Jesus.
- This step shouldn't be taken lightly, nor should the decision be made quickly. As Catholics, we believe that our faith develops and matures gradually, just as our physical, mental, and emotional lives mature over time.
- Adult baptism as a Catholic calls for **conversion**, a process of turning away from former ways of sin or self-centeredness toward grace and generosity, which comes to us through Christ. This doesn't usually happen in a single moment; it happens over time and with commitment. This is part of the reason the RCIA process was implemented—as a process of intentional preparation for adult baptism and the commitment to follow Jesus.

>>>
For more on how we understand baptism as Catholics, see the *Catechism of the Catholic Church*:

CCC: #386-421, 1212-1284

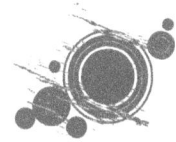

- **Is baptism for adults or infants**? The answer is "both," and "it depends."
    - In the Bible and in the first 200 years of Christianity, baptism was almost exclusively for adults. However, when the emperor Constantine converted to Christianity in 313 A.D., being Christian became fashionable instead of radical and dangerous.
    - Around the same time, St. Augustine developed the concept of **original sin**, which made infant baptism common.
    - Now that we emphasize the sacrament as a doorway into a community of faith, **Catholics welcome infants, children, or adults of any age to baptism**.
- So baptism:
    - **washes away our sin**,
    - makes us **adopted children of God**, and
    - makes us **members of the Body of Christ**.
- The Catholic church **recognizes baptism across Christian denominations**. Those who were previously baptized in another denomination are not baptized again.

YOUR BASIC BAPTISM

Exploring tough questions facing youth today

Baptism is…

- **A response to God's saving act through the life, death, and resurrection of Jesus Christ**
  (Acts 2:37-39).

- **An act of obedience to the teachings and example of Jesus Christ**
  Jesus was baptized, and the New Testament calls all who believe to be baptized
  (Mark 16:16).

- **A symbol of cleansing and new life**
  It is an outward sign of an inner experience. There is a new creation, a new birth
  (2 Cor. 5:17).

- **A public witness of the covenant relationship with God**
  Baptism is the sign of membership in the Christian covenant community (Eph. 4:4-6).

- **A commitment to become part of a witnessing Christian community, the body of Christ**
  Baptism is the moment of entering the church, of assuming responsible membership
  (1 Cor. 12:13).

- **A witness to the transforming power of the Holy Spirit in the believer's life**
  As they join the church through baptism, every Christian demonstrates an openness to the power of the Spirit (Rom. 12:2, Gal. 3:26-29, Eph. 4:5).

- **A beginning**
  It is understood not as something completed but as the start of a pilgrimage of faith
  (Romans 6:4).

Promises of Baptism

- Do you renounce Satan and all his works and all his empty promises?

- Do you believe in God, the Father almighty, Creator of heaven and earth?

- Do you belileve in Jesus Christ, His only Son, our Lord, who was born into this world and suffered for us?

- Do you believe in the Holy Spirit, the holy catholic Church, the communion of saints, the forgiveness of sins, the resurrection of the body, and life everlasting?

OR

- Do you believe in Jesus Christ as the Example of God's compassion who demonstrates the power of human connection and life as intended by God?

- Will you take your life pattern from Jesus, and will you learn his Way, repent of sin, receive God's forgiveness, and live in the light?

- Will you be loyal to the church, upholding it by your prayers and your presence, your substance and your service?

Permission is granted to photocopy this handout for use with this session.

>>> **SESSION 5**

YOUR BASIC RADICAL DISCIPLESHIP >>>

>>> KEY VERSES

Then [Jesus] said to them all, "If any want to become my followers, let them deny themselves and take up their cross daily and follow me. For those who want to save their life will lose it, and those who lose their life for my sake will save it." (Luke 9:23-24)

>>> FAITH STORY

Luke 9:18-27

>>> FAITH FOCUS

Jesus asked his disciples what people were saying about him, and then let out the inconceivable: that the Son of Man, whom some were calling the Messiah, would suffer and die. He was very
up front with all his would-be followers, telling them to count the cost of discipleship. But in his blunt challenge was also a heady, tantalizing promise: that some would not taste death before they saw God's loving realm. Framed by the stories of Peter's declaration and the transfiguration, this invitation to radical discipleship living is more attractive when we understand and experience who Jesus is.

>>> SESSION GOAL

Present participants with an invitation to discipleship as a way of life, a natural response of people who have given themselves to Christ.

>>> Materials needed and advance preparation

- Bibles
- Writing paper, pencils
- Copies of handout sheet for Session 5
- An edible snack that looks inedible (see Focus for a "recipe")
- Small (but not too small) inedible "treasures" to hide in the "snack" and extras for Respond
- Chalkboard/chalk and newsprint/markers
- Sofa
- Recordings (and player) of faith songs or hymns your group enjoys

TEACHING PLAN

1. FOCUS 10 minutes

Taste test: In order to get a "taste" of counting the cost of a life of discipleship, invite participants to decide whether or not to eat something that looks really unappealing. Concoct something edible that barely *looks* edible, enough for everyone to have some, and enough so that the requirement to finish it looks daunting. Example: big bowl of chocolate pudding with large pearl tapioca or pieces of gummy worms, a few leaves of wilted lettuce, maybe some olives. Or fix pig knuckles in a stew. Unidentifiable textures are a good idea. Make up your own. Have fun, and don't poison them! The main ingredient of the dish must be dark/

thick enough to hide a treasure buried in it. Hide something inedible: some coins, plastic egg with something in it, chocolate coins wrapped in gold foil, etc..

Conditions for the participants:

- *Decide **as a group** whether or not you'll eat this "snack."*
- *If you **do** eat it, **everyone** has to at least try it, and you have to commit to eating **the whole thing**.*
- *No utensils.* (Have washrags or wet wipes for afterwards, but don't let participants know you're prepared.)
- *No wasting it, throwing it away, or throwing it around.*

Suggest that they might make a list of pros and cons of the deal before making a final decision.

What happens if the group decides not to eat it? Then throw open the option of anyone eating it. If you still get no takers, find the "treasure" yourself and show them what they missed.

2. CONNECT 5-6 minutes

Choose discussion questions that are appropriate to what happened with your group in Focus:

- *Did anyone dive right in? Why or why not?*
- *Which conditions made you think twice? Why?*
- *How many of you "tasted" or tested just a little bit first? Why did you do that, if you knew you had to finish what you had started?*
- *Did you make a list of pros and cons? What made your decision for you?*
- *Would your decision have changed if you had known there was "treasure" involved?*
- *Did anyone feel as though they wanted to do something different from what the group decided? How so?*

Shift to the next activity by saying: *Like trying something that doesn't look very appetizing, it's wise to count the cost before diving into a life of discipleship. But you may also be surprised at what you find deep inside.*

3. EXPLORE THE BIBLE 10-12 minutes

Have participants search the scriptures listed below for clues to this question: *What do you think it is about Jesus Christ and his demanding way of life as described in the Bible that might have invited his followers to stick with him even though the outcome didn't look too appetizing at first and when it meant hardship, misunderstanding, humiliation, suffering, and even death?*

Divide into small groups and parcel out the passages as someone distributes copies of the handout sheet for Session 5. Direct participants to the question at the top so they can keep it in mind as they search. Suggest that they might again keep a list of pros and cons about following Jesus (on the handout sheet).

> Luke 9:18-22—Peter's confession of Jesus' identity
> Luke 9:23-27—The cost of discipleship
> Luke 9:28-36—The transfiguration of Jesus
> Luke 9:37-44—The healing of a boy with an evil spirit
> Luke 9:46-48—An argument over who will be greatest
> Luke 9:57-62—Some distractions in following Jesus
> Matthew 25:31-46—Separation of sheep and goats

"To deny oneself, as Bible scholar Lamar Williamson points out, is to acknowledge that we can never possess our own lives and can only find our true meaning, purpose, and fulfillment in the offering of our lives to the Messiah and to others.... It is precisely when we have nothing to lose that we have everything to gain."

Robbie Miller, campus minister

Have one person in each group record the group's answers to questions and share their group's conclusions with the larger group.

4. APPLY 10-12 minutes

Now that participants have "counted the cost" of discipleship, that is, looked at the pros and cons, have them do an activity that will require that someone actually "deny" him/herself for the sake of the group.

Crossing into discipleship. Have everyone line up at the end of a sofa. Tell them that they must work together to move as many people as they can across the sofa in 5 minutes.

Set these conditions:

- They may not go around the sofa, and they must cross it *lengthwise*.
- If anyone touches the sofa, that person cannot be counted in the total of people moved.

(If participants don't come up with a strategy within 5 minutes, suggest that one person be a "bridge" by lying face down on the sofa and letting others crawl across them.)

Then discuss: *How did you feel about sacrificing someone for the good of the group? How is this like Christian discipleship? Say more about what you think discipleship is really like. What does it look like? What does it mean? What does it cost us to do it? Or, what are some things we might "deny" ourselves in order to be disciples?* (See if the group can come up with specific instances or examples.) *What does it cost us **not** to do it?*

5. RESPOND 3 minutes

(If you have access to the recordings of the songs listed in Materials Needed, play them as you wind up the session with this final activity.)

Say something like: *There is spiritual treasure in a life of discipleship, even if it is costly. The _____ (whatever you had for treasure) I'm giving you is to symbolize the value of a life of discipleship, sometimes hidden deep inside. Keep it with you as a reminder that though discipleship may look risky, and may demand a lot, the pros outweigh the cons.* Give each person who didn't get some of the "treasure" from the "snack" earlier a piece of treasure for their own.

INSIGHTS FROM SCRIPTURE

Luke 9:23-34 is a "hard saying" of Jesus. It defies easy interpretation, and is not simple to carry out. It is a dangerous topic with themes of personal sacrifice, service in God's reign, and making hard choices. To follow God's leading, Jesus must go to Jerusalem and confront the religious and political establishment on their turf—at the temple and the palace. Jesus knows the consequences of this step. He will go from being a popular itinerant wonder-worker to a criminal convicted and killed for sedition against Rome. It will not be easy, glamorous, or triumphant—in the world's eyes.

> "Genuine love is demanding, but its beauty lies precisely in the demands it makes."
>
> St. John Paul II

> "Let us remember that love lives through sacrifice and is nourished by giving... Without sacrifice there is no love."
>
> St. Maximilian Kolbe

>>>

"Love falls to earth, rises from the ground, pools around the afflicted. Love pulls people back to their feet. Bodies and souls are fed. Bones and lives heal. New blades of grass grow from charred soil. The sun rises."

Anne Lamott,
Help, Thanks, Wow: The Three Essential Prayers

LOOK AHEAD

For Session 6 on community, you'll need some lively music suitable for a "musical chairs"-like game. One option in Respond asks for empty cereal boxes or cookie cartons for making postcards.

>> A MESSIAH WHO DIES?

Jesus asked his disciples what people were saying about him, and then let out the inconceivable: that the Son of Man, whom some were calling the Messiah, would suffer and die. He was very up front with all his would-be followers, telling them to count the cost of discipleship. The disciples of the first century understood "take up your cross" to mean, "Identify yourself publicly as a condemned person on the way to be crucified" (F. F. Bruce, *The Hard Sayings of Jesus*). As someone once said, "The immediate prospect of hanging wonderfully focuses the mind." Jesus is asking us to live our lives as if there is nothing more important than following him—his example and his instructions.

Later in Luke's account, Jesus interacts with several people who expressed interest in following him as he traveled toward Jerusalem. He challenged each one with the contrast between their other preoccupations (material comforts, family ties, and traditional responsibilities) and the demands of life with him. With such requirements for discipleship who would want to sign up? What convinced Peter, James, John, Andrew, Matthew, and the others to leave their families, jobs, and possessions to follow Jesus around the countryside, to a criminal's cross on a hill outside Jerusalem, and eventually (for many of them) to persecution and their own deaths? We must look to the remaining verses in this passage for the answer.

>> BECAUSE JESUS IS KNOWN

Framed by the stories of Peter's declaration and the transfiguration, this invitation to radical discipleship living is only reasonable when we understand and experience who Jesus is. Disciples can accept the invitation to the frightening and demanding *unknown* because *Jesus is known* to them. Knowing Jesus, both intellectually and experientially, becomes a larger part of our reality than the promise of deprivation and suffering. And when the disciples have committed themselves to him, Jesus intensifies their experience of himself—his past and future identity (in his transfiguration, vv. 28-36) and his present power (in his healing of the demon possessed boy, vv. 37-43).

Like Moses' call to leadership from the encounter with God at the burning bush in Midian (Exodus 3), the only thing powerful enough to commit us to the reality of discipleship is an ongoing encounter with Jesus Christ. Even in Jesus' blunt challenge was also a heady, tantalizing promise: that some would not taste death before they saw God's loving realm (Luke 9:27). Matthew 25:31-46 ("Lord, when did we see you hungry...") even implies that discipleship and service are such natural impulses of people who have given themselves to Christ that the people aren't even conscious of the expectation. Their service arises from their love.

>> POWER FOR RADICAL DISCIPLESHIP

Our covenant relationship with Christ requires that we will act in ways that are faithful to that relationship and trust in the promise that Christ will remain faithful to us. Jesus calls us to take up our cross and follow him. Through the gift of God's grace we are empowered to be disciples, filled with the Spirit, following not only Jesus' teachings but also his path through suffering to new life.

Your Basic Radical Discipleship

Exploring tough questions facing youth today

Search your assigned scriptures to "count the cost" of discipleship. If following the demanding Jesus Way means hardship, misunderstanding, humiliation, suffering, and even death, why do you think people stick with it? What convinced those first disciples to follow Jesus? Make a list of pros and cons about following Jesus. Add any that may not necessarily be found in the Bible.

PROS

1
2
3
4
5
6
7

CONS

1
2
3
4
5
6
7

Here is a list of the scripture references that will help you list pros and cons of following Jesus in a life of discipleship. If you finish yours early, try to find pros and cons in some of the others.

Luke 9:18-22—Peter's confession of Jesus' identity
Luke 9:23-27—The cost of discipleship
Luke 9:28-36—The transfiguration of Jesus
Luke 9:37-44—The healing of a boy with an evil spirit
Luke 9:46-48—An argument over who will be greatest
Luke 9:57-62—Some distractions in following Jesus
Matthew 25:31-46—Separation of sheep and goats

Discipleship.

What is it?
What does it look like?
What does it mean?
What does it cost me to do it?
What does it cost me *not* to do it?

Permission is granted to photocopy this handout for use with this session.

>>> **SESSION 6**

YOUR BASIC COMMUNITY >>>

>> **Materials needed and advance preparation**

- Music player with lively music suitable for "musical chairs"-like game
- Prizes for "Anatomy" winners (*optional*, see Focus)
- Writing paper, pencils
- Copies of handout sheet for Session 6
- Bibles
- Colored markers
- Cereal boxes or cookie cartons, scissors, one postcard for template

>> **KEY VERSES**

As the body is one and has many members, and all the members of the body, though many, are one body, so it is with Christ. For in the one Spirit we were all baptized into one body—Jews or Greeks, slaves or free—and we were all made to drink of one Spirit. (1 Corinthians 12:12-13)

>> **FAITH STORY**

1 Corinthians 12:4-27; Romans 12:3-21; James 1:19–2:17

>> **FAITH FOCUS**

Paul uses the metaphor of the human body to describe the kind of relationships God wants us to have with one another when we commit to following Jesus Christ. These scriptures are all about figuring out how to work together, worship together, meet each other's needs, and still respect individual identity and responsibility.

>> **SESSION GOAL**

In the midst of a world where everybody is out for themselves, help participants see the interdependence of the community of faith as a "basic" of being Christian.

TEACHING PLAN

1. FOCUS 8-10 minutes

Play "Anatomy." This is an elimination game like musical chairs. Some trinket—pencils, erasers, key chains, candy, etc.—shaped like a body part would be excellent prizes for the last few people in the game.

All the participants mill around the room at random while the music plays. When the music stops, call out the names of two body parts and a number (such as, "Foot to Forehead-3"). Everyone must *join themselves in groups of the number called with the mentioned body parts in contact*. The last people to do so are eliminated from the game and sit back to watch. The game goes on until all but one group is eliminated.

If you have a very small group, simply call out different combinations until people begin to tire of the activity.

2. CONNECT 3-5 minutes

Ask the group: *What was the strangest connection you made in this game? How did you feel when you couldn't find anyone to connect with? What was it like to turn "extra" people away from your group?*

Shift to the next activity by saying: *It isn't always easy to bring everybody together just the way we'd like. But that's not an excuse to give up. Being part of a faith community is basic to living as Christians.*

> "We cannot love God unless we love each other. We know Him in the breaking of the bread, and we know each other in the breaking of the bread, and we are not alone anymore... We have all known the long loneliness and we have learned that the only solution is love and that love comes with community."

Dorothy Day, co-founder of the Catholic Worker.

3. & 4. EXPLORE THE BIBLE / APPLY 20 minutes

Distribute handout sheets, divide into three small groups, and assign a scripture passage with its accompanying questions to each group. The *method* of this is a key part of its message: There is no way that one person or group can study all the passages in the time allotted. We need each other—our different perspectives, experiences, thoughts, feelings, abilities, and gifts—to grow as the Body of Christ. Each set of questions leads the groups into figuring how they might apply their passage. Come back together after 10-15 minutes and read key verses and report discoveries to the larger group.

The passages are 1 Corinthians 12:4-27 (varieties of gifts and the Body has many members); Romans 12:6-21 (instructions for using individual resources for the benefit of all); and James 1:19–2:17 (listening and doing, faith and works).

5. RESPOND 10-12 minutes

>> **Option A:** Create a **yurt circle** to demonstrate having to rely on someone else to help do something: Form a circle with an even number of participants. Have them stand facing the center almost shoulder to shoulder and holding hands. Choose one participant to start by saying the word "in"; the person to his/her right says "out." The next person says "in," and so on, around the circle. On the count of three the "ins" lean toward the middle of the circle, and the "outs" lean away from the center. Keep feet stationary. Participants should support each other with their hands. Encourage participants to see how far they can lean without losing their balance or breaking the circle. Return to the upright position.

Next ask the participants to lean in the opposite direction from what they did the first time—again on the count of three. Return to the upright position.

This time tell participants you will count to three several times and they should shift the direction of their leaning each time. (Begin with their first leaning directions.)

Note: The name of this activity derives from the Mongolian nomads' tent in which the roof pushes against the walls in perfect equilibrium, keeping the structure standing. (from *More New Games*)

>> **Option B:** Using a regular postcard as a template, cut out scenes or silly faces from empty cereal or cookie boxes (needs to be card stock) to make into postcards to send notes to people in the parish. Each participant writes to one person of their choice, expressing *why they are glad for that person's gifts in the congregation, or why they're glad they're part of the Christian community with them.*

>> **Option C:** Make a plan for the next time anyone from your youth group or even your parish is returning from a trip. As a group, surprise them at the airport, bus station, or train station to greet them. Take balloons, banners, flowers, anything to make them feel special, to demonstrate you're part of a supportive community.

INSIGHTS FROM SCRIPTURE

The Bible uses several different metaphors, or word pictures, to describe the kind of relationships God wants us to have with one another when we commit to following Jesus Christ. One metaphor that appears in many places in the New Testament is the picture of the community of believers being like a human body. These "body" scriptures are all about figuring out how to work together, worship together, meet each other's needs, and still respect individual identity and responsibility.

The themes that keep repeating themselves in these passages about life in community are:

1. A community of intersecting resources and needs is the only way to live as Christ's Church.
2. We have challenges as we attempt to live together as a believing community:
   - our individual human perspectives which make it hard to understand and to be understood
   - our cultural, socioeconomic, and family backgrounds which limit and prejudice us
3. The Holy Spirit is the One who will join us together and make us holy and whole.

ISN'T IT PERSONAL?

All believers must come to terms with the meaning of the good news in their lives and respond to Jesus' call to "follow me" in a personal way. Making the decision to follow Jesus has lifelong implications. It is necessary to be on this journey with other followers for on-going support and correction. Without this corporate dimension, faith becomes a private matter between God and me and loses the ongoing opportunity for God to work through the lives of other believers in ways that help me grow and follow more faithfully.

It's important that we not confuse a personalized faith with a private faith, writes Abe Bergen in *YouthGuide*. As Christians, we covenant to be accountable to one another in all of life. When we join the church, we are in essence saying, "I am willing to be accountable to this group of Christian believers for my Christian life and practice." We are also committing ourselves to supporting others and keeping them accountable to their Christian commitments.

MUTUAL ACCOUNTABILITY

Mutual accountability is a difficult practice to maintain in a society where the rights of the individual reign supreme. One way to live together in such a society is to say, "You believe what you want and I'll believe what I want, and I won't expect you to change as long as you don't expect me to change." While this may be an amicable solution for our society, it destroys the essence of church community.

In Matthew 18:15-20, authority is given to the church to discern right and wrong and hold one another accountable in matters of doctrine and conduct. Sometimes it's a delicate balance for a faith community to maintain accountability to its traditional understanding of what it means to be faithful and also honor prophetic messages that call us to new or difficult levels of discipleship.

"Two people, three people, ten people may be in living touch with one another through [God] who underlies their separate lives. This is an astounding experience, which I can only describe but cannot explain in the language of science.... It is as if the boundaries of our self were enlarged, as if we were within them and as if they were within us. Their strength, given to them by God, becomes our strength, and our joy, given to us by God, becomes their joy...the solid kernel of community of life in God is in the center of the experience, renewing our life and courage and commitment and love."

Thomas Kelly,
A Testament of Devotion

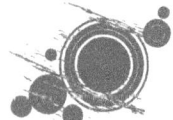

> "It's important that we not confuse a personalized faith with a private faith."
>
> Abe Bergen

There are lots of scripture passages about Christian community because there is nothing that we encounter that the first-century believers did not also struggle with. As you prayerfully read these chapters, ask the Holy Spirit to speak to your own heart about how and where you can grow. A critical question for you as leader is: Are you in a meaningful, committed community yourself? If not, how can you begin to be find or create this in your life? If so, what has this support and accountability meant in your own life? It is out of your own community experience (or lack, thereof) that you will have insight and the Spirit's empowerment to present this "basic" of Christianity—life in community.

> "In Louisville, at the corner of Fourth and Walnut, in the center of the shopping district, I was suddenly overwhelmed with the realization that I loved all these people, that they were mine and I theirs, that we could not be alien to one another even though we were total strangers. It was like waking from a dream of separateness… Then it was as if I suddenly saw the secret beauty of their hearts… the person that each one is in God's eyes. If only they could all see themselves as they really are. If only we could see each other that way all the time. There would be no more war, no more hatred, no more cruelty, no more greed… But this cannot be seen, only believed and 'understood' by a peculiar gift. "
>
> Thomas Merton
> *Conjectures of a Guilty Bystander*

Your Basic Community

In Real Life
Exploring tough questions facing youth today

Being part of a faith community is basic to living as Christians. After you know which of these scripture passages you'll be studying, do three things:

- Discuss the questions associated with your passage.
- Choose three verses from your passage that you believe are the "heart" of it. You'll read these to the large group when you give your other suggestions, so they'll know what you're talking about! Can your small group agree on which three?
- Make two concrete suggestions for how your group can demonstrate the "heart" of this message to your parish. This could include suggestions for naming gifts or how we can build up the body of Christ.

1. **1 Corinthians 12:4-27:** All the gifts of the Spirit are necessary. How does this passage help us to understand the role of both unity and diversity? What are some of the ways our youth group or our parish represent diversity of gifts? (List specific gifts that correlate to Paul's list, but also gifts such as leading music, playing a specific instrument, fixing meals, mediating fights, making bulletins, telling stories. How about diversity of needs? (List them: physical, emotional, monetary.) Diversity of perspectives?

2. **Romans 12:6-21:** This passage lists specific instructions on how to live for the benefit of each other, using individual resources for all. How should we act toward one another? How does each of these actions benefit the giver as well as the receiver?

   Apply what you've discussed to this situation: Paula is pastoral associate in a large and diverse urban parish. God's Spirit has blessed the members of this parish with many spiritual gifts. It is a very exciting place to be. Usually.

   Right now, two groups in the parish are complaining, loudly, to Paula. One group thinks music sung or played at mass should be done as perfectly as possible. Only the very gifted musicians in the parish should play the organ or sing in the choir and only older, traditional songs should be used. (This group does not want guitars or drums played at all.)

   The other group thinks music sung or played at mass should be the best a person can do, but not necessarily perfect. This way older children, youth, and average musicians could contribute to the liturgy; more people could be involved. Also, this group would like to see a wider range of more contemporary music played. (This group thinks using guitars and drums would be a good idea.)

   How would you help them mediate this problem?

3. **James 1:19–2:17:** List all the practical things in this passage that you think are critical to living with other Christians. How should the rich and the poor look at life as members of the same community? Suggest specific ways for this to happen. What does this passage say about knowing ourselves and being honest with ourselves? What is God's attitude toward "saving seats" (favoritism)? Imagine a hermit, who never sees anyone, doesn't read the newspaper, and is totally isolated. Is it possible for that person to be a Christian if s/he never has contact with a faith community? Why or why not? What teachings in this passage would a hermit be unable to live out? Can you think of other teachings found elsewhere in the Bible that a person who never had contact with a faith community would find difficult to live out? (Examples: feed my sheep, love one another, love your neighbor as yourself, wash one another's feet, communion, praying for others because you never know their joys or needs.)

Permission is granted to photocopy this handout for use with this session.

>>> EXTENDER SESSION

>> **Option A** (best used after Session 1 or 2)

>> SESSION GOAL

Understand the Jewish celebration of liberation by participating in a modified Seder.

>> PLAN

A Seder Supper is a feast held on the eve of Passover, the 8-day observance commemorating the freedom and exodus of the Israelites (Jewish slaves) from Egypt. Jewish families usually celebrate the Passover meal in their homes. The meal uses food as symbols of the events around the exodus, and has a long tradition. Consider inviting a Jewish person to lead your group in a seder service. You can download a printable service (http://scheinerman.net/judaism/pesach/haggadah.pdf) or create your own using a Seder how-to wizard (http://www.chabad.org/library/howto/wizard_cdo/aid/120432/jewish/Introduction.htm). As with the Shabbat service in Session 2, remember that this is a *Jewish* prayer, and part of the Jewish sacred tradition. It is important to take your lead from your Jewish guest as to how to go about this in a way that is respectful of the tradition.

Option: Consider organizing a Seder as an event for the whole church to experience.

After you participate in the Seder, discuss what you have experienced.

- *What did you learn about Judaism in this experience?*
- *What did you learn about Christianity in this experience?*
- *What did you experience in your own relationship with God?*
- *What new understanding do you have of the concepts of liberation, covenant, and commitment?*

>> **Option B** (best used after Session 5 or 6)

>> SESSION GOAL

Hold a footwashing service (or other similar symbol) to demonstrate another basic of Christian life—service.

>> PLAN

There are many levels of meaning that can surface from a footwashing service:

- Following the example of Jesus (John 13:5-20) who performed the servant's job of washing the dirty feet of his followers before their Passover meal is one way to demonstrate our recognition of Jesus' command that we love and serve one another. In Jesus' day, people were barefoot or wore sandals and walked on dirt paths, so their feet would be dusty, tired, and perhaps sore or injured. Providing servants to bathe a guest's feet was a way that a generous host could show hospitality (sort of like providing fresh towels in the bathroom or putting a bowl of fresh flowers in the guest room). Jesus was the host and he provided a vivid example to his followers by taking the servant's role with them as well.

>> **Materials needed and advance preparation**

- **Option A:** Seder or Haggadah service and food (see sources listed)
- **Option B:** Basins, towels, warm water, music and player (optional) for footwashing

- Pages of instructions are recorded in the Hebrew Law for ceremonies of washing that demonstrated obedience and devotion to God. Beyond personal hygiene and health, ceremonial washing is sacred preparation to appear before God.

Give youth some of the above background, concluding with, *Jesus tells us in John 13:14 that we should wash each other's feet as he has washed our feet. So that's what we will do. It might seem vulnerable or embarrassing or humbling, but there's something special that can happen to us as we serve each other in this way.*

Extend the involvement of participants in this footwashing service by having them help you with the preparations: getting the towels, filling basins with warm water, etc. You may choose to have them do this in silence, communicating only with touch and gestures. You'd break the silence by passing the peace after washing feet (see below).

Then instruct the group in your church's footwashing procedure—don't assume they know it—and if your church does not regularly practice footwashing, or has no standard way of doing it, follow this procedure:

Separate the girls and the boys into two circles if this will reduce any tension. Otherwise, have the whole group sit in chairs in a circle and explain the procedure. Have everyone take off shoes and socks.

Begin by kneeling down before the person on your right and washing both feet. This is not a thorough washing, just a gentle wetting and drying of each foot. After you have dried both feet, both of you stand up and hug each other. You might want to say "Christ's peace" or "Christ be with you," or choose not to say anything. Pass the towel on, and then this person kneels down before the person on his or her right and so on.

Your feet (the leader's) will be washed last. After your feet have been washed, call for a group hug and close in prayer.

Alternatives: Choose another symbol of service to each other, akin to washing feet, and follow the same procedure as for the footwashing, substituting your own symbol. This could be washing of each other's hands or even cleaning the church restrooms!

CLUELESS AND CALLED
Discipleship and the Gospel of Mark

What does it take to be a disciple? This study of the Gospel of Mark focuses on the requirements for following Jesus' way and the abundant life that is ours as a result. (5 sessions)

DO MIRACLES HAPPEN?
Signs and Wonders in the Gospel of John

The greatest miracle, recorded in John 1:14 and 3:16, is the miracle of God's love that became flesh and lived among us. But John also included examples of what we more traditionally think of as miracles: the wonder of abundance from little; healing; signs of impossibility and faith; and the resurrection. (5 sessions)

DO THE RIGHT THING
Ethics Shaped by Faith

How do you know what's right and what's wrong? Even when you figure it out, the right thing is often the unpopular or unpleasant choice. This unit offers participants a clearer sense of what it means to claim a faith identity, a foundation that can help them sort out the gritty details of ethics shaped by faith. (6 sessions)

FIGHT RIGHT
A Christian Approach to Conflict Resolution

This unit will help youth understand conflict and its function. They will learn how they can be honest and loving, and explore how conflict can be used for positive results. They will also learn ways to enhance their communication skills. 1 Corinthians. (5 sessions)

GOD IS A WARRIOR?
Violence in the Bible

The Bible challenges us to be reconciled to one another and work for justice. So what do we do with the stories that seem to condone violence or even encourage it? A discussion of issues in the Old and New Testaments. (6 sessions)

HOW DO YOU KNOW?
Wisdom in the Bible

Wisdom literature teaches us that we gain knowledge of the world, ourselves, and God through experience and observation. This unit provides practical, hands-on wisdom to help young people avoid life's snares and grow closer to God. Proverbs, Job, Ecclesiastes. (5 sessions)

HOW TO BE A TRUE FRIEND
The Bible Reveals Friendship's Heart

To be a friend takes skill. Help youth discover the secrets of friendship through various stories from the Old and New Testament. (6 sessions)

HOW TO READ THE BIBLE
Building Skills for Bible Study

What kind of book is the Bible? What does this book mean to me? This unit looks at the Bible as revelation, as history, as literature. Selected scripture. (5 sessions)

KEEPING THE GARDEN
A Faith Response to God's Creation

If Christians believe that God made the world, we do not need any more compelling reason to care for it than that God has handed us a treasure to hold and protect. This unit gets beyond trendy environmentalism and challenges youth to see environmental awareness as a religious issue. Genesis. (6 sessions)

MANTRAS, MENORAHS, AND MINARETS
Encountering Other Faiths

How is Christianity different from other faiths? Why do others believe the way they do? This study can give youth a new appreciation for the uniqueness of Jesus. Selected scripture. (5 sessions)

SALT, LIGHT, AND THE GOOD LIFE
The Beatitudes and the Sermon on the Mount

What can youth expect in a life of discipleship? This unit explores the Sermon on the Mount under four main sections: the Beatitudes, Salt and Light, Jesus and the Law, and Heavenly Teachings. Matthew 5. (6 sessions)

A SPECK IN THE UNIVERSE
The Bible on Self-Esteem and Peer Pressure

Discover God's unconditional love and acceptance of all people. This study will show positive ways to have one's life make a difference, and help youth find ways to resist negative peer pressure and turn it into positive action. (6 sessions)

THE RADICAL REIGN
Parables of Jesus

Jesus used parables to reveal what the kingdom of God is like, and how God relates to us. This study highlights how the parables reveal God's reign as radically different from the world we live in, and what that means for the Christian life. (6 sessions)

TESTING THE WATERS
Basic Tenets of Faith

Discover the biblical roots for the central Christian concepts of covenant, community, and baptism. This short course is a way to test the (baptismal) waters of Christianity before diving in, or review the basics for those who already have. (6 sessions)

WHO IS GOD?
Engaging the Mystery

God is beyond human comprehension, yet desires to be known. These sessions focus on the way we get clues about and glimpses of God from the Bible, God's creation, and church tradition. Selected scripture. (5 sessions)